Mouths
Are for Smiling

THE SENSE OF TASTE

Katherine Hengel

Consulting Editor, Diane Craig, M.A./Reading Specialist

A Division of ABDO
ABDO
Publishing Company

visit us at www.abdopublishing.com

Printed in the United States of America, North Mankato, Minnesota
102011
012012

 PRINTED ON RECYCLED PAPER

Editor: Liz Salzmann
Content Developer: Nancy Tuminelly
Cover and Interior Design and Production: Oona Gaarder-Juntti, Mighty Media, Inc.
Photo Credits: BananaStock, Digital Vision, Shutterstock, Thinkstock

Library of Congress Cataloging-in-Publication Data
Hengel, Katherine.
 Mouths are for smiling : the sense of taste / Katherine Hengel.
    p. cm. -- (All about your senses)
 ISBN 978-1-61783-199-7
 1. Mouth--Juvenile literature. 2. Senses and sensation--Juvenile literature. I. Title.
 QL857.H46 2012
 612.8'7--dc23
                             2011023494

SandCastle™ Level: Transitional

SandCastle™ books are created by a team of professional educators, reading specialists, and content developers around five essential components—phonemic awareness, phonics, vocabulary, text comprehension, and fluency—to assist young readers as they develop reading skills and strategies and increase their general knowledge. All books are written, reviewed, and leveled for guided reading, early reading intervention, and Accelerated Reader® programs for use in shared, guided, and independent reading and writing activities to support a balanced approach to literacy instruction. The SandCastle™ series has four levels that correspond to early literacy development. The levels are provided to help teachers and parents select appropriate books for young readers.

| Emerging Readers (no flags) | Beginning Readers (1 flag) | Transitional Readers (2 flags) | Fluent Readers (3 flags) |

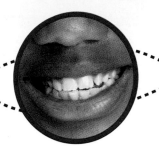

Table of Contents

Mouths

Are for Smiling

We use our mouths to smile. Antoine smiles at his **classmates**. He makes them laugh because his smile is **magnified**!

What else are mouths for? What can mouths sense?

Mouths

Are for Tasting

George licks an ice-cream cone. He bought it from an ice-cream truck in his neighborhood. It tastes sweet! It is cold too.

The roof of your mouth is covered with **taste buds**. So is your tongue! Taste buds send messages to our brains. That's how we taste things!

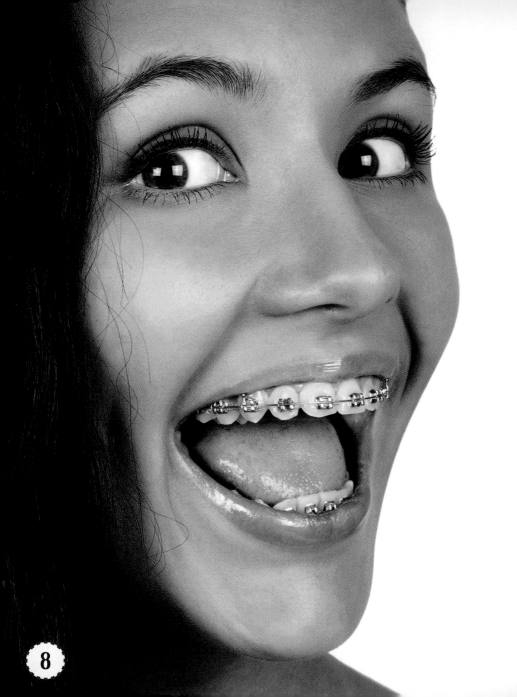

Our Sense of Taste

Taste is one of our five senses. Taste helps us sense the things we eat.

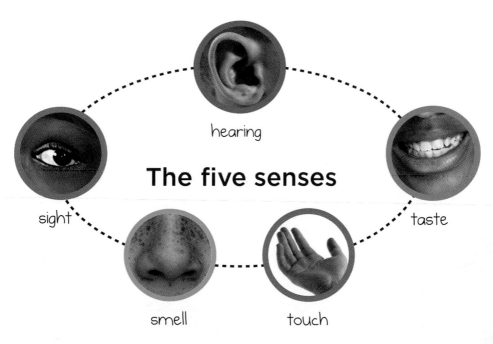

hearing

sight

The five senses

taste

smell

touch

Mouths
Are for Apples

The Ramos family goes on a **picnic**. They have apples and **sandwiches**. Peter eats his apple first. He likes apples! They taste sweet.

Mouths

Are for Lemons

Maria tastes the lemon. Her sister dared her to do it! Maria makes a funny face. The lemon tastes really sour!

Our mouths tell us if something is sour, spicy, sweet, or salty.

Mouths

Are for Pizza

Everyone's tastes are different. Each person has a **unique** sense of taste. Amber thinks the pizza is very spicy. Anna doesn't think it is spicy at all!

Mouths can do a lot!
What else can mouths do?

Mouths

Are for Kisses

Samantha loves her aunt. They go to the park on Sundays! Samantha gives her aunt a kiss on the cheek.

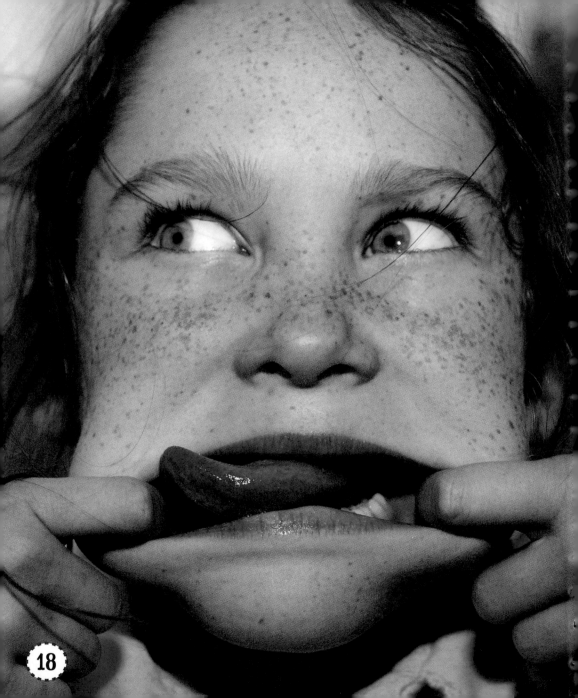

Mouths

Are for Funny Faces

Tanya knows how to make a funny face. It drives her older brother nuts! But Tanya's friends think it is really funny!

Mouths
Are for Blowing Bubbles

Adeena uses her mouth to blow bubbles. She's blowing very carefully. She wants to blow the biggest bubble she can!

Facts About Taste

◆ We have about 10,000 **taste buds** inside our mouths.

◆ Girls usually have more taste buds than boys.

◆ The way something tastes has a lot to do with how it smells.

Taste Quiz

1. The roof of your mouth doesn't have **taste buds**. True or false?

2. Taste is one of our five senses. True or false?

3. Everyone's tastes are exactly the same. True or false?

4. Samantha and her aunt go to the park on Sundays. True or false?

Answers 1. False **2.** True **3.** False **4.** True

Glossary

classmate – a student who is in the same class as you.

magnify – to make something look larger than it is.

picnic – a meal eaten outdoors, often while sitting on the ground.

sandwich – Two pieces of bread with a filling, such as meat, cheese, or peanut butter, between them.

taste bud – one of the tiny bumps in the mouth that sense what things taste like.

unique – different, unusual, or special.